Lynn Erichson

CREATIVE CANVAS WORK

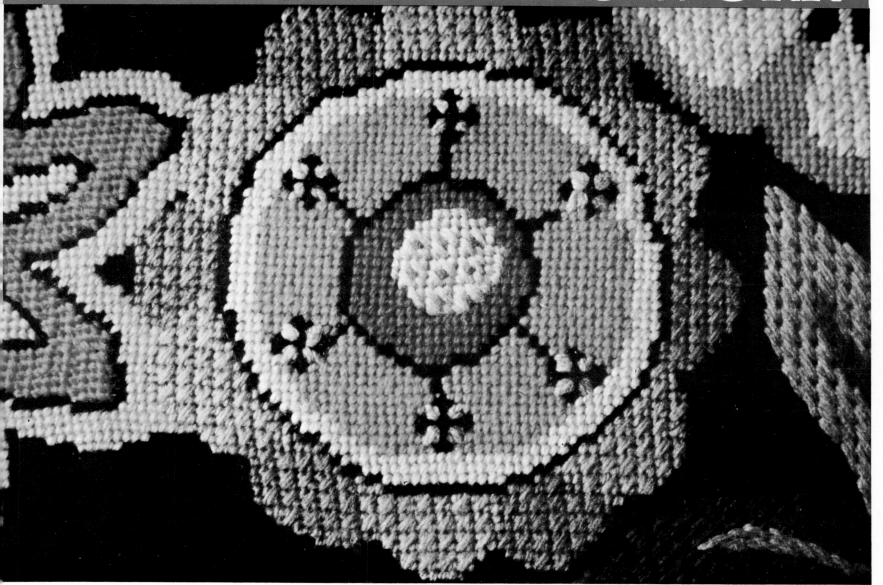

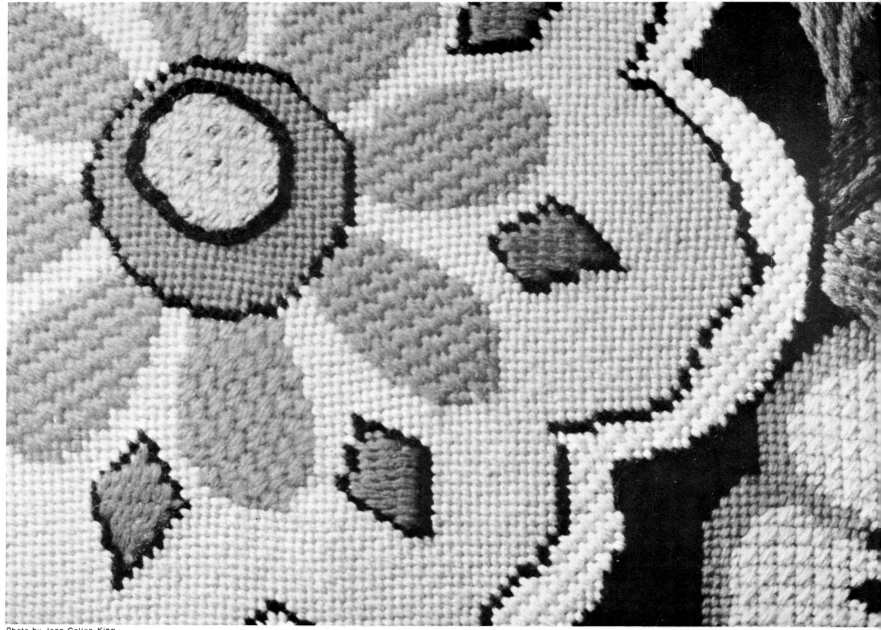

Elsa S. Williams

CREATIVE CANVAS WORK

VNR VAN NOSTRAND REINHOLD COMPANY
NEW YORK CINCINNATI TORONTO LONDON MELBOURNE

This book is dedicated to my granddaughters

Julie and Lisa

and to grandchildren everywhere, who will become the needleworkers of tomorrow.

Van Nostrand Reinhold Company Regional Offices:
New York Cincinnati Chicago Millbrae Dallas

Van Nostrand Reinhold Company International Offices:
London Toronto Melbourne

Library of Congress Catalog Card Number: 74-141443

Designed by Myron S. Hall III. Printed and bound in Tokyo, Japan by
Zokeisha Publications, Ltd. Color photography by Malcolm Varon and
Slide House. Other photographs by George H. Boyer. Published by Van
Nostrand Reinhold Co., a Division of Litton Educational Publishing, Inc.,
450 West 33rd Street, New York, N.Y. 10001.

Published simultaneously in Canada
by Van Nostrand Reinhold Company Ltd.

1   3   5   7   9   11   13   15   16   14   12   10   8   6   4   2

Acknowledgments

This book was encouraged by the questions and enthusiasm of my
associates and thousands of professional needlecrafters who pro-
mote my products. I am deeply indebted to them for their partici-
pation in the American renaissance of needlework.

I especially want to thank Ellen Rae Kaufman for creating the
beautiful chair shown on page 35 and for her designs and needlework which appear on pages 17, 20, 37, 38, 39, 40, 41, 42, and 43. My
thanks also to Phalice Ayers for her fine example of mitered
Bargello shown on page 8.

The repeat designs on page 52 were copied from an antique sampler loaned to me by my friend Martha Davenport. Claire Schrock
capably executed my teaching sampler shown on page 32.

My gratitude also is extended to Barbara Klinger, who skillfully
edited this book.

Photo by Jean Callan King

CONTENTS

INTRODUCTION

The art of needlework on canvas is perhaps the most challenging and most versatile of all forms of embroidery. Its final value often exceeds that of any other completed needlework and the satisfaction of accomplishment is unlimited.

I am frequently asked what my favorite needlework is and my answer usually is, "That which I am presently doing." It is true that I am fascinated by all handwork and find it exciting to see a design develop with needle and thread. This is especially so when forming a leaf or petal in beautiful crewel wools on linen, but it is also possible to create these same effects on canvas. Surface stitchery usually depends on the fabric to provide the background, but in canvas work an additional challenge presents itself because the background must also be completed by the needleworker and the background is often as creative as the design.

The finished work shown in color on page 9 of this book is an example of how you can combine crewel and tapestry wools in surface stitchery before working an interesting needlepoint background. Other examples for combining surface embroidery stitches with canvas-work stitches are pictured within the book to entice you to use all your embroidery skills and to develop new ones in creative canvas work.

Many designs, however, do not adapt to a combination of stitches. Some of the most beautiful canvas-work pieces have been accomplished entirely with the slanting Tent Stitch. This is the basic needlepoint stitch which can be worked in any of three different ways — as the Half Cross Stitch, the Continental Stitch, or the Diagonal Basket Weave Stitch. The beginner should become acquainted with these three stitches

before beginning any canvas work. All three look alike and can be used to create the design on the canvas; but each of these stitches is constructed differently and each has its own purpose depending upon the design and the canvas to be worked. More information on these stitches will be found in Chapter 5.

Before beginning to work on canvas it is important to understand the word "needlepoint." This is an accepted, general name for all Tent Stitch canvas work. The suffix word "point" comes from the French word meaning stitch. In Italian this word is *punto* and in Portuguese it is *ponto*. All, of course, mean only stitch and needlepoint is therefore needle-stitch. This is what canvas work is all about. It is making stitches with a needle. Work on fine canvas with mesh that requires 16 or more stitches per inch is called petit point, which means small stitches. Canvas work on mesh which permits 8 to 15 stitches per inch is usually considered gros point, meaning large stitch. Very large stitches, worked on canvas with 3 to 7 mesh openings per inch, produce "ponto grado," which is the Portuguese term for "large stitches."

Because Tent Stitches, when evenly spaced and smoothly worked, give the appearance of woven cloth, the term "needlepoint tapestries" was used to distinguish needle-stitched pieces from loom-woven tapestries. When this needle art developed into practical application, the word "tapestry" was omitted and all such work is now generally called needlepoint. The term "canvas work" includes needlepoint and all stitchery and embroidery which is worked into canvas.

Opposite:
"Field Bouquet" was designed and worked by the author on #13 white mono-canvas. Crewel yarns are combined with tapestry yarn. Flowers and leaves were worked first and background was completed later with canvas-worked Tent Stitches.

This Bargello design has four sections mitred against a background of Tent Stitches. Begun in the center, the design was worked outward in four directions to the edges. Needleworked by Phalice Ayers. Many Bargello patterns can be worked from four sides, creating unusual effects for pillows.

"Carrousel" is a canvas-worked sculpture mounted into a standing, boxlike frame. The shadows at top and left are needleworked in blending tones to increase the dimension of the shadows caused by lighting effects. The brass ring, a symbol of good luck and eternal happiness, hangs from the top by a strand of tapestry yarn and creates additional shadows in the bright yellow square. The motion of the carrousel is depicted with surface stitches in red, orange, and gold.

1. MATERIALS AND TOOLS

All canvas work requires three essential materials which should be chosen with consideration for the desired effect. The canvas, the yarn or thread, and the needle must all be of related size. A needle that is too large will spread the holes of the mesh and distort the canvas. A needle that is too small will cause excessive pressure on the yarn as it is pulled through the mesh and will cause it to fray, especially if it is pulled through rough canvas. Like an oversized needle, if the yarn is too thick, it also will distort the canvas when it is forced through the mesh and will result in a very crooked piece. At the other extreme, thin yarn on large-meshed canvas produces a piece with canvas threads showing. Consequently, it is very important to have the right materials and tools.

Canvas

Canvas is available in many qualities. Do not attempt to put your time and effort into cheap canvas which results in worthless projects. The same effort and skill can produce heritage needlework when good canvas is purchased for a small additional cost. You can test the strength of the canvas by tearing it. If it tears easily it is not suitable for chair seats or any item requiring mounting. Avoid all canvases which have a dull finish from starch or inferior cotton threads. These rough materials cause the yarn to fray and are difficult to work because they require more force to pull the thread through the starched holes. Good canvas work deserves canvas made from strong, polished thread.

Single-thread canvas, called mono-canvas, is available in several sizes. For most pieces, I prefer canvas with 13 mesh to the inch because it allows good detail and it is easy to see each thread that forms the mesh. This is especially helpful when it

is necessary to count threads. It is interesting to observe that very old pieces were often worked on this size canvas, indicating that it was one of the standard sizes available more than a century ago.

When researching material for the book *Bargello* (Van Nostrand Reinhold, 1967), I discovered that tan cotton-and-jute mono-canvas produced the best results. For this type of canvas work it is important to have coarse, rough threads to hold each stitch in its vertical position. The polished threads of white mono-canvas are not suited to this Florentine canvas work because it permits the yarn to slide through the mesh, forming tight stitches which show the canvas threads and the stitch holes.

In mono-canvas, mesh is formed by single threads.

Duo-canvas is woven with two threads for each mesh. The threads are woven in pairs both horizontally and vertically. The spaces between these threads provide the holes in which to stitch. This is the canvas you will find used for most pieces of ready-worked needlepoint. When sections of the design are to be done in petit point it is possible to separate the two threads in order to have both petit point and gros point on the same canvas. Four stitches of petit point are worked where the threads cross instead of a single stitch in regular gros point.

There are other advantages provided by duo-canvas, and there are some occasions when mono-canvas cannot be used at all. For example, when working a design in Tramé, it is necessary to sew a foundation of parallel threads before working

Duo-canvas has a mesh of double threads.

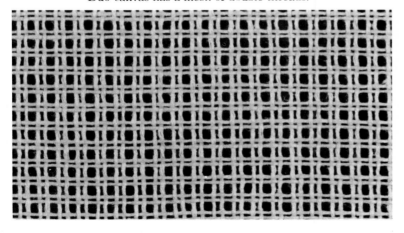

Traméd design has thin, colored yarns stitched in parallel lines between double threads as a foundation for canvas-work stitches, which are placed over the established design.

This "Blue Delft" design is an excellent example of how crewel embroidery can be used on canvas work. The centers of the flowers are embroidered with French Knots. The white background is worked in the Basket Weave Stitch.

Twelve strands of crewel yarns are used in every stitch of this carpet. It will last for hundreds of years because of these strong threads and the evenly worked Tent Stitches. Combining threads of several colors produced the unusual effects in this carpet.

13

If you purchase a ready-worked design be sure to use a tapestry yarn of equal quality for the background. This motif appears in the finished carpet at right.

This carpet was worked in four strands of tapestry wool on 5-to-the-inch duo-canvas. Each square was completed separately and then joined to form the carpet.

the final, decorative stitches. These Traméd lines are always sewn between the two threads of duo-canvas. And, while I make an effort to discourage its use for all needlepoint, it should, however, be mentioned that the Half Cross Stitch must also be worked on duo-canvas. Continuous Cross Stitches also require two or more threads to hold them in position and duo-canvas is usually chosen for this. However, it is possible to form Cross Stitches on mono-canvas if you sew over two threads of the canvas.

The most popular duo-canvas used is woven for 10 stitches per inch, but it is also available in very large sizes for ponto grado work. Small mesh duo-canvas, which is woven from fine cotton thread, produces a soft base for appliqué and items for wearing apparel.

Yarns

All the designs and pieces shown in this book have been worked in tapestry yarn or crewel yarns. My opinion on yarns has been influenced by my observations of museum pieces and by personal experience. While I often admire a piece that has been created from various other wools and threads, I am nevertheless concerned with encouraging heritage embroidery and therefore believe that, if you have chosen to work a beautiful design on good canvas material, the work also requires the best yarn you can purchase. The following are my recommendations.

The size of the canvas will determine the thickness of the

yarn which you are to use. If it is to be very fine work, you will want to use crewel. Genuine crewel yarn is a strong, twisted, two-ply yarn which is made from long fibrils of wool. The choice of colors in crewel is almost unlimited. For petit point and areas requiring surface embroidery, the single, two-ply thread of crewel is excellent. Multiple strands of crewel are excellent for gros point if you can keep an even, smooth tension on your work. I have seen beautiful needleworked carpets which were worked with twelve strands of crewel on 5-mesh-to-the-inch canvas. These multiple-strand carpets, made with strong crewel yarns, have lasted for hundreds of years.

Beautiful effects in crewel canvas work can be achieved by mixing colors. For example, if you wish to create the illusion of a sea or a sky in motion, you can begin with three strands of a dark shade of blue and gradually replace one thread with a lighter strand until the coloring is very, very light. The carpet on page 13 was worked with a blend of deep maroon and bright red strands to create a middle tone and a combination of tan, gray, and white threads to make a soft oatmeal-tan.

Tapestry yarn for gros point should be chosen with care. The length of the wool fibril determines the quality of the tapestry yarn. It is false economy to use a knitting worsted or any short-staple yarn for work which should have lasting value. If you have purchased a piece with the design already stitched by the renowned Madeira needleworkers, you will notice that it is worked with a beautiful, soft, velvety yarn. Therefore, I believe that your background work should be done in the same yarn to give the entire piece a smooth, even appearance. Many expensive and elegant pieces of needlepoint have been massacred with shiny, hairy yarn or with tapestry wool that was too thick for the canvas.

The tapestry yarn which is best for completing a stitched design is not heavy and it should be worked loosely to allow for lofting of the yarn. This four-ply yarn is twisted to increase its strength, but it is not as hard a twist as is formed for so-called background tapestry yarns. Because the twist is soft, several strands of this yarn can be blended for needleworked carpets in the same manner as I have described for using crewel yarns.

To create beautiful pieces of canvas work it is often necessary to have several shades of one color. If you choose a yarn which is available in at least five shades of a color to work a flower or leaf you can create very realistic effects.

A recent addition to tapestry threads has been the development of a non-tarnishing metallic thread suitable for canvas work. This thread is soft and flexible due to its crochet-like construction, and the strong polyester strands pass through the canvas without breaking. Beautiful highlights can be achieved with this new thread, and its flexible construction makes it possible to use it for petit point as well as gros point.

Needles

The success of your work depends in a large measure on the needle you use. A good test to determine the correct size is to pass the unthreaded needle through the canvas. If it falls through the mesh smoothly without force from your fingers, it is usually the right size. Then, test it once again using the yarn or thread in the needle. Work a small section of canvas to decide if the threaded needle requires you to tug at each stitch. If the yarn is very heavy it may be that you will need a thinner needle so that the combined thickness of the needle's eye and the yarn can fit through the mesh. Because the double thickness of yarn at the eye of the needle will fray from constant abrasion on the canvas, it is important to choose the correct needle to fit the yarn. In addition, if you have to use force to pull the needle and thread through the canvas, you will disturb the tension of your work. This is especially true when stitching background areas where smooth, evenly worked surfaces depend on an even tension.

At first it may seem difficult to thread a thin needle with yarn, but one soon discovers that it is worth the effort because it makes stitching easier and faster. This is my method for threading yarn into the eye of a needle: Place the cut end of the yarn between the thumb and forefinger of your right hand. Press these fingers together firmly, concealing the end of the yarn. Aim the eye of the needle where you know the yarn is and force the needle eye between your tightly pressed fingers. The yarn will slide into the eye of the needle. This takes a little practice at first, but I believe that it is easier than the method of threading folded yarn.

Sharply pointed needles are not usually successful when working stitches which must pass through the holes of the

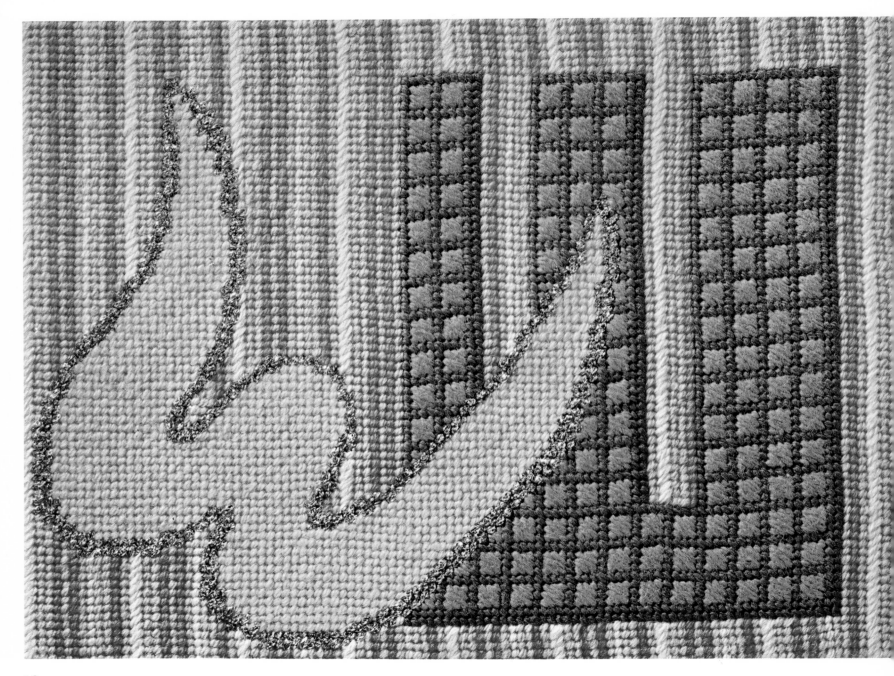

16

Facing page:

Initials and letters can be the basis of design in canvas work. By combining a variety of stitches to create texture and by choosing a pleasant color scheme it is possible to create a pictorial monogram. The initials "EW" can be viewed either vertically or horizontally. The background letter is shaped in Scottish Stitch squares to provide an angular contrast to the curved letter. Continental Tent Stitches were worked in varied tones and widths to create the striped background.

This fret pattern can be increased in size to a large piece for a beautiful pillow. Rows of flat stitches surround both the center motif and the band motifs, which are worked in Tent Stitches.

canvas because the point can split the yarn threads of the preceding stitches in the design. It is much better to work with a standard tapestry needle with a dull, rounded point. My favorite needle is size 22 for canvas with 10 to 14 mesh per inch, using medium-weight tapestry yarn.

When a design requires surface stitchery such as crewel embroidery, it is necessary to use a crewel needle. These needles have long eyes and they are sharply pointed, making it possible to stitch into the canvas threads as well as into the holes of the canvas. For surface stitches requiring heavy yarns, you may wish to use chenille needles, which also have sharp points.

Now that you know what kind of needles to use, be careful to purchase only the best quality needles, ones that are made well rounded and also well polished. Be sure to keep your needles in a moisture-proof container or in a piece of wool felt if you live in a damp climate. An old English needlework scrapbook had written in it, "A dull needle worketh a worried stitch," and I have indeed found this is true. Needles cost very little so treat yourself to a fresh supply when yours become dull and do not slide through the canvas with ease.

Scissors

For taking out stitches a good pair of small, sharp-pointed embroidery scissors is essential. Small, because you want a short distance of blade to aim at the stitch and large scissors may accidentally cut the canvas. Sharp-pointed because you will want to cut only one stitch at a time. Use the point to lift the stitch before cutting it on the right side of your work and to pull the ends of the thread to the wrong side. Never cut on the wrong side of your work because you may cut into other stitches or disturb ends of other threads.

Canvas Frames and Rods

For working the design area of a canvas piece it is often very helpful to use a frame. Wooden frames are available in many sizes and they include dowel sticks that turn to roll and unroll the canvas, which is attached to them with tape. Very large frames suitable for carpets are available on floor stands.

A small or a medium-sized canvas can be conveniently mounted on artist's canvas stretchers, which are sold in art supply shops. Larger pieces can be worked in this manner if the frame is placed on a table so that part of it projects over the table's edge and the remaining part is held firmly to the table top with a heavy weight. With one side of the frame weighted to the table, you can keep one hand above the extended canvas and one hand below it as you work.

A recent invention which we have developed is the needlepoint rod. It consists of a lightweight, slotted tube with one closed end. The canvas edge is slipped through the open end of the rod and into the horizontal slot, and the canvas is then rolled around the rod to the point where the needlework is to be done. Two sharp pins are used to hold the canvas in place.

This simple device is a great aid in working background areas for it holds the canvas threads in place and prevents distortion. At the same time it permits making a complete stitch in one motion, which speeds up the work. Because the hand holding the rod is always in contact with the wrong side of the work instead of the designed side, this method also keeps the needlepoint unsoiled. Another advantage of the rod is the convenience in handling needlepoint while working in a plane, a car or in your favorite, comfortable chair.

For working a large design area, two rods can be used to hold opposite sides of the canvas with only a portion of the design area unrolled in the center. This is especially helpful when working Bargello, which usually needs to be started in the center of the canvas.

A needlepoint rod prevents canvas distortion and keeps the work clean.

If you feel uncertain about your ability to design your first piece of creative canvas work, there are hundreds of beautiful ready-worked designs available for you to purchase in fine needlework shops. Working a plain, solid-colored background provides a feeling of tranquility and a sense of accomplishment as the piece progresses. However, these same ready-worked canvases can be used more creatively if you invent your own interesting background effects and borders. The photographs on page 22 show three finished canvas pieces which were created by adding shadows and borders to ready-worked pieces. This is an excellent way to begin.

Background shadows are created simply by counting the stitches of the design. Using a slightly darker shade of the background color, the shadow is worked by counting 6 threads to the side and 6 threads below the design or 6 threads above it depending on the design. Continue working the shadow, where the canvas is vacant, to conform to the pattern outline.

Beautiful borders are created by varying the tones of the color and by changing the stitch. Continuous Cross Stitches, Double Star Stitches, Leviathan and Herringbone Stitches are all excellent for this purpose. Experiment on the edge of your canvas until you find the effect you like best. If you have chosen to use a stitch which covers several threads of the canvas, it is important to count the number of threads beginning at the center of each side so that all corners will come out evenly spaced. Page 23 shows several of these borders, which are fascinating to work.

The choice of a background color for the design is very important because it can brighten or soften the colors in the design. One should always avoid choosing colors which are similar to the colors on the edges of the design because this disturbs the design form and creates a monotonous tone.

For many years only solid-colored backgrounds were used, but with the present enthusiasm for creative canvas work many pieces are being worked with interesting background stitches and subtle tones of blending colors. There are unlimited possibilities for creating exciting backgrounds. However, it is important to mention that one should always choose a background which complements the design and the design should always be larger than the background area. Page 21 illustrates how a rose blossom with green leaves can be affected by various background colors and shadows.

Tramé and Painted Canvas

These same interesting shadows and borders can be added to Tramé or painted canvas pieces which are available for those who wish to work the entire piece from a pattern that is already prepared by a professional designer. Tramé has the design worked in long horizontal threads which are sewn on duo-canvas. These pieces are usually sold with matching yarn to complete the design. Painted designs on canvas present more opportunity for accomplishment than Tramé. When purchasing a painted piece it is important, however, to choose only pieces which are carefully painted with flexible ink or paint on good canvas. Avoid heavily stenciled designs which can dry and crack inexpensive cotton canvas. These pieces are not deserving of your efforts.

A delightful treatment of a simple design, this piece was worked for me by Ellen Rae Kaufman. Encroaching Gobelin stitches form the tomato and the remainder is worked in Tent Stitches with Parisian Stitches in the border.

Facing page:
The same rose design is shown with four different backgrounds.
Lower left: The rose on the white background is very clear. It resembles a painting on plain white paper. If a crisp effect is desired, white or light colors are excellent.

Upper left: When this same rose has a black background, the tones of color in the design appear to be darker and the design blends into the canvas work without losing any of its detail.

Upper right: A shadow worked in two tones of light gray can be an effective way to produce a beautiful background. This is done by counting the stitches of the design and duplicating the motif in the background area. This effect was achieved by counting 6 threads to the right and 6 threads toward the bottom of the canvas. From this point the design is copied stitch for stitch.

Lower right: This section was worked to illustrate the wrong way to create a shadow. Here the deep shades of gray are confusing the design. Since both daylight and artificial light usually come from above, it is unnatural to have the shadow placed above the design and it creates a disturbing effect.

Ready-worked designs can be used creatively by adding backgrounds and borders of your own choice.

A floral pillow illustrates how shadows and an interesting border enhance a ready-worked design. Above it is a handbag with white daisies on a gold background with deep gold shadows.

Left:
Vase of flowers is worked entirely in Tent Stitches. The colorful blossoms have an unusual dimensional effect because of the shadows and the pattern worked into the background.

Facing page:

MONOCHROMATIC BORDERS

Upper left: Center area is worked in Mosaic Stitch and the border is in four shades of Scottish Stitch. By alternating the direction of the border stitch, additional texture is achieved.

Upper right: Tent Stitches are used for the center area and are repeated on the dark, outside edge. The rows of Double Star Stitches which make this beautiful border are done in four shades of one color.

Lower left: The Cross Stitches around the outside edge have dark areas of Tent Stitches placed between the scallops to accent the border. Remainder of the canvas is worked in Basket Weave Tent Stitches using the lightest shade of yarn, and Cross Stitches are worked on top of the Tent Stitches. Working stitches on top of the finished background gives an added dimension and texture to the border.

Lower right: Center area is completed in Diagonal Mosaic. Varying widths of Tent Stitches produce the bands of the border. Changing the size and the direction, as well as the color tones, of these satin bands will produce very unusual borders. The outside edge is created by combining Tent Stitches with Mosaic squares to match the texture of the center panel.

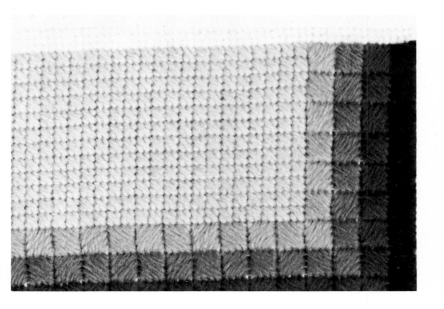 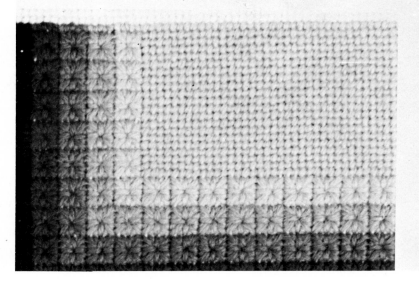

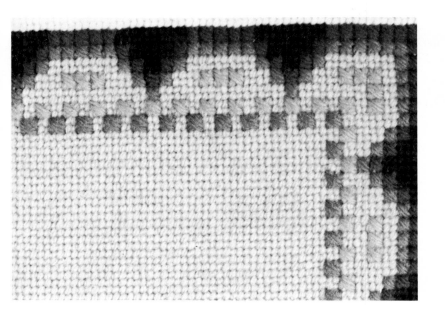 

23

3. CREATING YOUR OWN ORIGINAL DESIGN

This cloisonné footstool design was adapted from the beautiful Chinese cloisonné vase. Gold threads outlining each motif re-create the appearance of the brass edgings in the original enamel work. This is an excellent example of what can be achieved with paper patterns placed to produce a handsome, overall design. (The patterns used are on page 26.) Designs of this type are best worked in smooth Tent Stitches and would lose the effect if worked in textured stitches.

The sketch at the left was the inspiration and guide for the needlework piece shown here.

If you draw and paint well, you have unlimited joys to experience in canvas work. It is possible to create almost any design or scene with traditional needlepoint. Of course, delicate and intricate detail depends in a large measure on very small, carefully worked stitches. However, the amateur artist can create beautiful pieces, too, by adapting a design from an ornamental object or from paintings and illustrations. A visit to a museum can provide inspiration for many designs.

For novices who have no art training, it is best to begin in silhouette or solid form and then gradually progress to simplified, shaded motifs. Begin by making a pillow to match a wallpaper pattern, or design a chair seat using a motif from drapery material. If the design is complicated, you can trace a section and enlarge it into a beautiful design.

When drawing an original design, a few basic rules should be remembered. Keep the design as simple as possible. Do not divide the canvas with a center line. The principal motif is usually best when placed below the center and slightly to one side, except when the design is intended to be symmetrical. The background area should complement the design and should not exceed the size of the design.

Beautiful canvas work designs can be formed from cutout paper patterns. Flowers, leaves, butterflies, or geometrical forms in simple, paper patterns can be placed on the canvas and moved about until a pleasing design forms. These pieces are then pinned in position and an outline of each paper pattern is drawn on the canvas in waterproof ink. A felt-tipped pen is excellent for this. The cloisonné footstool and the cloisonné handbag shown on page 26 were both designed in this way.

Whatever method you choose, remember that the designing of the canvas always continues throughout the working of the piece. It is often necessary to change a line or shape to accommodate the weave of the canvas or the choice of stitches. Therefore, it is usually best to work the entire design before beginning the background.

Artistic ability expands the possibilities of needlework as in the example above, but novices can create beautiful designs from simplified forms, using cutout paper patterns. The cloisonné handbag was done in this manner. The patterns here can be traced and then enlarged with graph paper.

In cases where it is not desirable to use cutout patterns, the design can be painted directly on the canvas with waterproof acrylic paints or with permanent oil paint mixed with Japan drier and turpentine. Whatever material you use, it must be applied in liquid, not paste, form. If the paint is thick, it will clog the mesh of the canvas and these solids will rub off on the yarn. If too much medium or glaze is mixed with the paint, it can also fill the canvas holes and disturb the position of the stitches. Of course, all painted canvases must be thoroughly dry before they are worked and all must be colorfast.

It is often more gratifying to work the design without painting the color scheme on the canvas. If you have enjoyed the creative accomplishment of crewel embroidery, you know the satisfaction of developing beautiful color effects on a design which was only an outline pattern. My favorite method for preparing an original design for canvas work is very similar. I find an outline drawing permits more freedom than a painted canvas, though a colored sketch is helpful for reference.

First, paint the design or picture on paper in the same size as you have planned your needlework. Whenever possible, paint on paper in the same colors as the yarn or thread you intend to use. When the colored sketch or painting is completed, make a separate outline tracing of the design, drawing only the essential details. This tracing may be used for making a perforated pattern to stamp the design on the canvas.

To perforate the paper you need to pinprick it or use a perforating tool on the lines of the design to get your pattern. After perforating the paper pattern, place it on the canvas and hold it in position with weights. Rub the entire design area of the paper with a felt pad (such as a blackboard eraser) which has been dipped in colored pattern powder. The powder should pass through the holes of the paper and appear as an outline of the design on the canvas. Remove the paper pattern carefully to avoid spilling the powder and spotting the canvas. Spray the canvas design area with alcohol to set the pattern powder and keep it from rubbing off as you stitch.

If you do not wish to make a perforated pattern, it is possible to trace the outline drawing onto the canvas with a felt-tipped pen containing waterproof ink. A light table made with frosted glass is very useful for this step in the process of preparing the design, and white canvas is easier to use for this method. The pattern for tracing needs to be drawn clearly in black ink because a penciled drawing will not show through the canvas. Place the canvas on top of the tracing and make an outline drawing directly on the canvas.

The needlework is now created by following the original painting or drawing as a color reference for shading and detail. The outline drawing on the canvas is the guide for the placement of the yarn colors. This method of working is less confusing than trying to match colors on a painted canvas and it is a joy to see the design develop on the plain canvas.

It is also possible to use graph paper for drawing a design if you do not mind counting the little squares. Graph diagrams are excellent for mottos and samplers requiring evenly spaced letters and for repeat designs. When planning the patterns for graph paper, it is important to consider that slanted Tent Stitches create a narrow, firm line when worked diagonally from left to right and a semi-detached, wide line when worked diagonally from right to left.

Mottos and other pieces requiring even spacing can be planned first on graph paper.

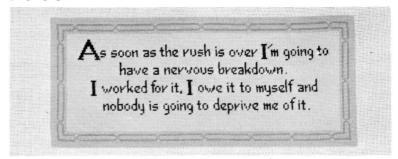

As soon as the rush is over I'm going to have a nervous breakdown. I worked for it, I owe it to myself and nobody is going to deprive me of it.

It is easier to work a design in needlepoint from a simplified sketch or drawing rather than from a photograph or detailed painting. Compare the treatment of the oil painting at the upper left with the pleasant, flat tones of the water color below. It would have been very difficult to transfer all the detail in the oil painting. The water color, which I painted several years later, became the inspiration for the needlepoint picture "Brewster Mill" on the opposite page. The canvas work was done following an outline drawing on the canvas and the water-color sketch was used for color reference and shading.

5. CHOOSING STITCHES

When the design is ready to be worked, which means the pattern has been transferred to canvas, the color scheme has been planned and the yarns and threads have been chosen, it is necessary to decide what stitches will be used. Most designers and artists form mental patterns of textures as well as patterns of design and color. Creative canvas work provides many opportunities for interesting textured effects.

For pictures and ornamental objects, it is possible to use a variety of large stitches to create textured effects, but for chair seats, pillows and objects requiring wear or abrasion, it is best to avoid large, loose stitches.

The importance of using the diagonally worked Basket Weave Tent Stitch for upholstery and chair seats cannot be stressed too strongly. This flexible bias stitch for solid areas will produce a piece which will last for centuries while all Half Cross Stitches and Continental Stitches can last only as long as the canvas remains unbroken. Everyone who desires to produce good canvas work should master the Basket Weave before attempting any others.

The choice of canvas stitches depends in a large measure on one's personal preference. There are many good needlework dictionaries and magazine references to follow for stitch construction, but it is always essential to choose fancy stitches wisely. A beautiful design can be ruined with too many different stitches.

While smooth stitches are usually worked into backgrounds, there are several other textured stitches which can create lovely effects when the texture does not interfere with the design. The stitches shown on page 31 are worked over four threads of canvas. They can be very effective worked in one shade but are illustrated here to suggest possible combinations of shading in three or more tones.

Top Row, left to right:
1. The Scottish Stitch pictured is worked in squares with all stitches slanting in the same direction. Shown here worked diagonally, it can also be worked horizontally and vertically for borders or checkerboard effects.

2. The Alternating Cashmere Stitch is worked diagonally with the alternate rows slanting in the opposite direction of the preceding row. The Cashmere Stitch is usually worked with all stitches slanting in one direction, but the alternating version produces less canvas distortion.

3. The Double Star is a beautiful border stitch. The short V-stitches at the side of each center stitch produce a neat, flat design. Each square consists of 16 stitches but only the first 4 and the last 4 are sewn into the center canvas hole.

4. The Fly Stitch is similar to the Lazy Daisy embroidery stitch. The stitch is tied down at the bottom of each open loop. It must be worked from top to bottom to create the smooth ridges in the canvas.

Lower Row, left to right:
1. A Scottish Stitch with Diagonal Mosaic. The solid squares in Scottish Stitches and broken rows of Mosaic are worked diagonally. One row of Mosaic is worked on the opposite diagonal with stitches keeping the same slant.

2. The Parisian Stitch resembles the Bargello or Florentine Stitch because all the stitches are sewn vertically. The long and short stitches sewn in horizonal rows adapt well to produce shading effects.

3. The Jacquard Stitch has rows of long stitches alternating with rows of short stitches and produces a pleasant texture. It is usually seen in one tone of color but can be effective when worked in several shades.

4. Tied Oblong Cross Stitch. This elongated stitch is tied in the center with a crossbar. Each row is worked horizontally with alternate rows spaced between the rows above and below.

1 2 3 4

1 2 3 4

For centuries people have worked unattractive little swatches and squares as samplers to keep a record of their stitches. This piece was designed to provide teachers and beginners with a practice piece that can be enjoyed forever. All the solid areas of this design may be worked in a variety of stitches. The black background provides sufficient area to learn the accomplishment of smooth Tent Stitches worked in Basket Weave.

Facing page:
Semi-precious stones from Brazil and India were inserted into the design by constructing a setting of buttonhole stitches in gold cloisonné thread. The first row of buttonhole stitches was worked into the canvas. Succeeding rows were stitched into previous rows. After stones were inserted each row was pulled tighter until the stones were held securely. Gold cloisonné thread was also used to work the outline of the design in a combination of Tent Stitches, Cross Stitches, and various sizes of Pyramid Stitches. The flat areas of the design were all smoothly worked in Tent Stitches, with the contrast of colors producing dimension and action in the design. Upper background is completely covered with Cross Stitches; lower foreground in Basket Weave Stitches with two shades of color in alternating rows. This effect was achieved using two needles, each threaded with a different color. Left panel is a solid area of alternated Scottish Stitches.

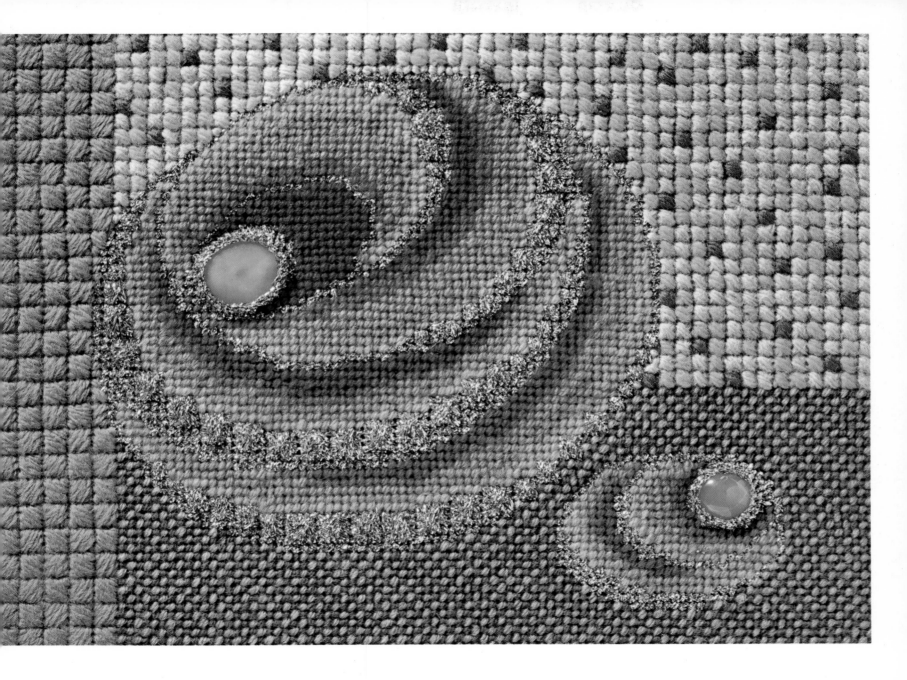

The tree trunk is worked in Outline Stitches; background trees and mountains in Florentine Bargello Stitch; foreground in Cross Stitch; sky in Basket Weave Stitch; leaves in slanting Tent Stitches of various lengths. Entire piece is worked in black, white, and gray on #13 white mono-canvas.

In addition to the many canvas-work stitches, there are all the decorative surface-embroidery stitches such as French Knots, Outline, Long and Short, Chain, Satin, Herringbone, etc., which can be applied to creative canvas work. The creative possibilities in canvas work are unlimited.

On the following pages are seven designs, each worked in a variety of stitches and each accompanied by an outline drawing with a numbered key showing which stitch was used in each area of the design. Become familiar with the way each stitch looks and refer to these examples when working out the stitches according to the diagrams on pages 44 to 50.

This canvas-worked chair by Ellen Rae Kaufman was embroidered in a combination of many stitches against a solid Tent Stitch background. These beautiful motifs are all based on circular forms. Enlarged sections of similar motifs appear on the following pages.

Overleaf:
Compare the results achieved using the same design and colors. Both sections have the same Tent Stitch background worked on #13 white mono-canvas. The panel at the right was completely done in tapestry yarn. The panel at the left has flowers worked in crewels. Flower petals are embroidered in Long and Short Stitches with French Knot centers.

1. Basket Weave Stitch
2. Cross Stitch
3. Rice Stitch
4. Slanting Gobelin
5. Tent Stitch
6. Scottish Stitch
7. Diagonal Mosaic
8. Diagonal Mosaic with woven bars
9. Cashmere Stitch
10. Surface Chain

To delineate the pattern it was best to work a row of Tent Stitches around most of the sections. The surface Chain Stitch is not traditionally done on canvas but was used here to raise the petals of the flower form where they became lost against the other motifs.

Background #1

1. Byzantine
2. Tent
3. Milanese
4. Smyrna Cross

The Byzantine Stitch gives the background of this design a motion resembling that of water. With this choice of background stitch it was best to work most of the design in Tent Stitches. Four shades of blue-green cause the leaves to blend with the water and add to the stitch effect.

. Scottish Stitch
. Tent Stitch
. Upright Gobelin (with crossbars)
. Cross Stitch
. Variation of Scottish Stitch
. Traméd Gobelin
. Double Cross Stitch

or best results the background should be
vorked first so that the Scottish Stitches of
he design will be in line with those in the
background.

he Scottish Stitch variation in the lower-
eft motif has a small stitch couching down
he long center thread. This small stitch is
vorked in the opposite direction from the
cottish Stitch and in a different color yarn
o attract attention to this detail.

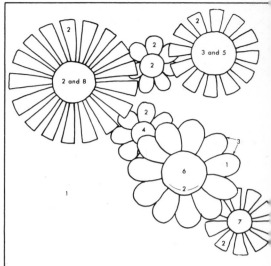

1. Cashmere Stitch
2. Tent Stitch
3. Tent outline
4. Gobelin
5. Star Stitch
6. Double Cross Stitch
7. Knotted Slant Stitch
8. Laid Work with French Knot

It is best to work the Cashmere Stitch back ground first before working the design. Th will make it possible to align the stitches the rounded petals which are worked Cashmere Stitches. All other motifs are ou lined in Tent Stitches. The Laid Work wit French Knots is embroidered on top of th Tent Stitches.

1. Upright Gobelin (over three threads)
2. Upright Gobelin (over two threads)
3. Tent Stitch
4. Double Star Stitch
5. Cross Stitch
6. Double Cross Stitch
7. Knitting Stitch
8. Fern Stitch
9. Chain Stitch
10. French Knot
11. Scottish Stitch
12. Rococo Stitch
13. Triangle Stitch

Notice that this design was worked *on the diagonal of the canvas,* a #13 white mono-canvas. That is why the slanted Tent stitches look upright and the Gobelin stitches look slanted. The entire background was worked first so that the Scottish stitch of the large motif could be in line with it.

1. Upright Gobelin
2. Chain Stitch
3. French Knots
4. Long and Short
5. Tent Stitch

The design was worked first by stitching directly into the canvas holes. French Knots were stitched over one thread of the canvas and Chain Stitches were spaced evenly following the curves of the leaves. The entire background was worked in Upright Gobelin Stitches with diagonal Tent Stitches covering the corner of each row.

1. Tent Stitch
2. Scottish Stitch
3. Cross Stitch
4. Diagonal Mosaic
5. Encroaching Gobelin
6. French Knot
7. Single and Double Tent
8. Rice Stitch
9. Web Stitch

This was designed as a beginner's piece and is used in many classes to introduce the canvas worker to a few interesting stitches which can later be used on more challenging designs. Notice that it is necessary to change the direction of the Encroaching Gobelin Stitches when working the leaves. The Web Stitch is made by stitching diagonal threads across the section to be covered. Then overcast Tent Stitches are spaced alternately to create the effect of woven fabric.

6. STITCH DIAGRAMS

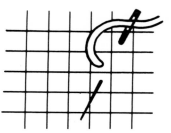 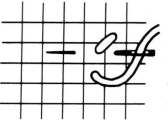 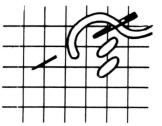 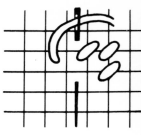

BASKET
WEAVE
STITCH

1. This step makes first stitch and begins second stitch. Start at top right corner of area to be worked.

2. This makes second stitch and begins third stitch.

3. This makes third stitch and begins fourth stitch. Needle must be at this angle to end the rows at upper left side.

4. This makes fourth stitch and begins fifth stitch. The needle must be vertical and parallel to canvas threads. (Fifth stitch, not diagrammed, is made in same way.)

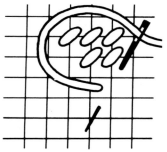 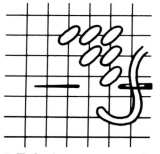 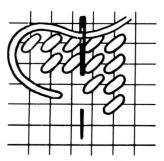 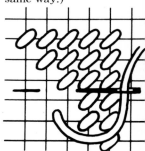

5. This makes sixth stitch and begins seventh stitch. The needle must be at this angle to end the rows at the lower right side.

6. To begin a new row working right to left the needle must be horizontal and parallel to the canvas threads.

7. Work all left to right rows with needle placed vertically and parallel to canvas threads.

8. Work all right to left rows with needle placed horizontally and parallel to the canvas threads.

  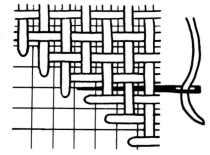

9. The reverse side of the work will have a woven effect resembling that of a wicker basket.

10. When ending threads, slide needle under the basket weave keeping needle parallel to the weave.

11. To begin a new thread, slide needle under the basket weave at right angles to the thread previously ended. This prevents thickness forming in one row.

44

←

Basket Weave Stitch (Tent Stitch)

It is extremely important to encourage canvas workers to use this stitch when working in solid areas. This stitch, which is worked on the diagonal, prevents distortion and ridges which can occur when working horizontally and vertically. It provides a soft, flexible finished piece which is very desirable for upholstery work. Because the yarn is applied diagonally, it reinforces the weave of the canvas. Pieces worked in this manner last many years longer than those worked in Continental or Half Cross Stitch because it produces no strain on the canvas.

For best results use a small needle which will fall through the canvas holes without being pushed through. A number 22 tapestry needle is best for sizes 10 to 15 mesh. The correct weight of yarn is also important because heavy yarns will spread the canvas holes. Lightweight, lofted tapestry yarn does not require the stitches to be pulled tight and permits soft stitches which produce beautiful, smooth effects.

Beginning at the upper right-hand corner of the area to be worked, follow diagrams 1 through 6. Increase one stitch at the end of each row until you have attained the maximum width. All rows worked from left to right are worked as in diagram 7. All rows worked from right to left are worked as in diagram 8.

Notice that the needle is always parallel to the canvas threads except when ending or beginning a new row. The needle is always under two threads when working on mono-canvas and under two sets of double threads when duo-canvas is used. Every stitch lies diagonally over the cross-weave of the canvas.

CONTINENTAL STITCH

Continental Stitch (Tent Stitch)

This stitch is primarily used for lines and small areas. Because these backstitches are worked along a single row of threads, their durability depends on the strength of the canvas, and the Continental Stitch is, therefore, not recommended for chair seats or upholstered items intended to have long wear. Continental Stitch backgrounds frequently have ridges and distortion of canvas. This is why many needleworkers prefer to use the Basket Weave Stitch.

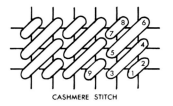

CASHMERE STITCH

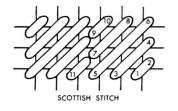

SCOTTISH STITCH

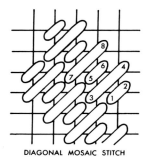

DIAGONAL MOSAIC STITCH

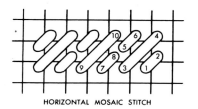

HORIZONTAL MOSAIC STITCH

Cashmere Stitch

Stitching from right to left, this stitch may be worked in rows or it may be accomplished diagonally. It is a beautiful background stitch. When the stitches are slanted in opposite directions every other row, this is called Alternating Cashmere. Odd numbers indicate where the needle has emerged from the canvas; even numbers, where the needle has been inserted. Step 8 ends the first Cashmere Stitch and step 9 begins the second in a horizontal row.

Scottish Stitch

A very popular background stitch which covers the canvas quickly, the Scottish Stitch may be worked in rows or diagonally. Interesting effects are achieved by working one square in one direction and alternate squares in the opposite direction. This stitch creates handsome effects when worked in rows of blending tones and colors. Step 11 begins the second Scottish Stitch.

Diagonal Mosaic

The Mosaic Stitch is best when worked diagonally. It produces a beautiful background effect which works up rapidly. This stitch is excellent for chair seats, upholstery, and objects requiring a flexible material for mounting. To increase the diagonal stripe effect, it is sometimes worked in two shades of the same color yarn, alternating the color every other row.

Horizontal Mosaic

For variation, the Mosaic Stitch can be done horizontally, which results in square areas of stitches. Compare this stitch with the Scottish stitch.

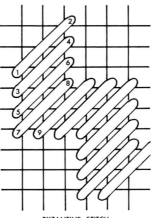

BYZANTINE STITCH

Byzantine Stitch

These long, diagonal stitches may be arranged in any number to achieve the zigzag effect but the construction is usually done in groups of 4 stitches passing over three threads of the canvas. If a row of Tent Stitches is worked between each row of Byzantine Stitches the stitch is called the Jacquard Stitch.

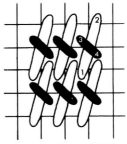

KNOTTED SLANT STITCH

Knotted Slant Stitch

The stitch may be worked horizontally or vertically. It is very effective when worked in two colors using one color for the slant and another for the stitch which crosses the slant.

Continuous Cross Stitch

It is important to have the top stitches all slanting in the same direction to achieve an even texture. This stitch is excellent for backgrounds and borders. It must be worked over two or more threads. Because of its square formation, it is also a good stitch to use for lettering. Each cross is completed before going on to the next stitch. This produces a better stitch than the method of working across a row in one direction and reversing to form the cross.

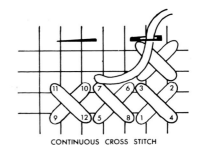

CONTINUOUS CROSS STITCH

Tied Oblong Cross Stitch

When this stitch is used for backgrounds, it creates evenly spaced ridges caused by the raised crossbars. All crosses must be made in the same direction but every other row is spaced to produce alternating bars. This is accomplished by stitching into the canvas hole between the crosses of the previous row. This stitch must be worked in horizontal rows.

TIED OBLONG CROSS STITCH

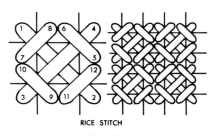

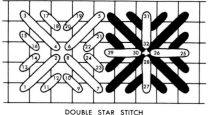

RICE STITCH

DOUBLE STAR STITCH

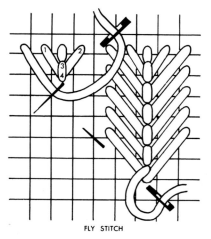

FLY STITCH

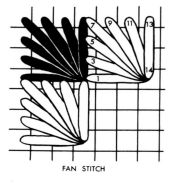

FAN STITCH

Rice Stitch

This beautiful stitch is slow to work but a rhythm can be developed if the stitches are worked according to the numbered diagram. Unusual effects can be achieved with this stitch when the squares are worked in checkerboard colors or when the first 2 stitches of each section are worked in a darker color.

Double Star Stitch

The first 4 and the last 4 stitches are sewn into the center. Side stitches form four V-shapes. This stitch is excellent for borders when worked in a continuous row. To create a beautiful, wide border of Double Star Stitch use four shades of tapestry wool working from light to dark. The pansy pillow on page 22 is an excellent example of the effect that can be achieved with a Double Star Stitch border.

Fly Stitch

This must be worked from the top down. For solid areas it is best to stitch the row on the right side first and progress toward the left. This stitch is excellent for borders and it produces attractive stripe effects when the color is changed in each row.

Fan Stitch

All stitches that form the fan are stitched into one hole of the canvas, working from left to right. This novelty stitch is recommended only for special effects. It is best for pictures and pieces which do not require wear. Note the use of Fan Stitches on the fish shown opposite.

Opposite:
The fascination of this design is that the fish are repeated by counting the same number of stitches in parallel rows to create the outline of each form. The solid areas of the fish bodies are worked in Tent Stitches with Double Cross Stitches sewn on top to create the raised spots, and the tails are worked in Fan Stitch. The interesting background is achieved entirely with slanted Tent Stitches carefully placed diagonally across the canvas in random width stitches.

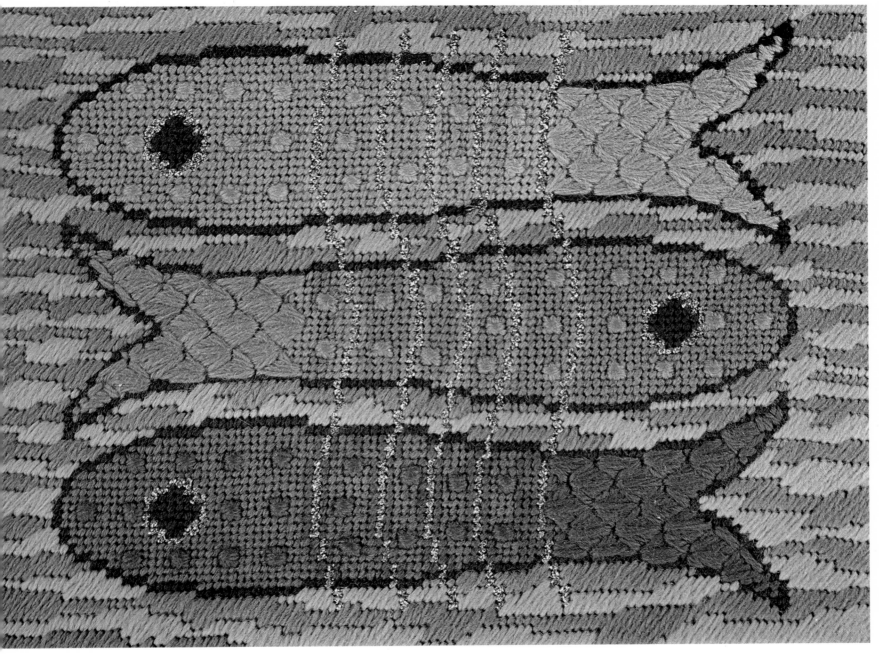

49

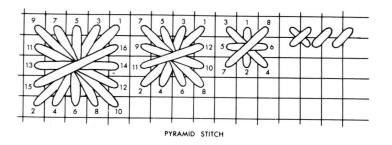

PYRAMID STITCH

Pyramid Stitch

Highly decorative, this stitch may be worked over any number of threads in a square formation and diminished to a Cross Stitch ending in a Tent Stitch. All top stitches in the formation should slant in approximately the same direction as the Tent Stitches, but it is best not to use the longer diagonal stitches for top stitches when the squares are very large. Rows of Pyramid Stitches form beautiful borders, creating a raised effect. This stitch has a high center which produces beautiful highlights when worked in metallic effects.

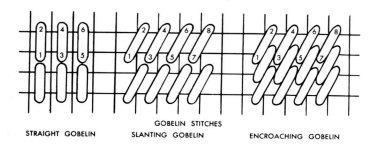

STRAIGHT GOBELIN   GOBELIN STITCHES   ENCROACHING GOBELIN
SLANTING GOBELIN

Gobelin Stitches

Straight or Upright Gobelin requires a lofted yarn to cover the canvas threads. If yarn does not cover the canvas, Traméd threads must be laid horizontally before the rows of upright stitches are worked.

Slanting Gobelin produces a woven effect and is often used to create copies of old tapestries. Every stitch slants across one vertical thread and over two or more horizontal threads.

Encroaching Gobelin can be worked over two threads or may be elongated to cover several threads if the canvas mesh is compatible with the size of the yarn.

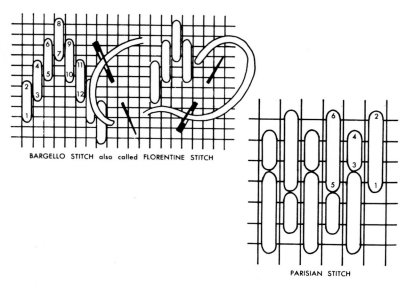

BARGELLO STITCH also called FLORENTINE STITCH

PARISIAN STITCH

Bargello or Florentine Stitch

All stitches are placed vertically on the canvas. Left side of diagram shows position of needle when progressing upward. Right side of diagram shows position of needle when advancing downward.

Parisian Stitch

This may be worked from right to left or from left to right. All stitches are parallel to the canvas threads and are worked in horizontal rows. This stitch produces lovely blending effects when worked in rows of several shades of the same color.

Beautiful effects can be created by using repeat designs, and there are many applications for their use in both overall patterns and border designs. All repeat designs can be used on either fine or coarse canvas and they may be created in colors to accommodate personal taste.

Many avid embroiderers keep several needlework projects in work at the same time. One of these is very often a repeat design. Perhaps this is because most creative people do not like the monotony of repeat designs and prefer to work on them a little at a time. However, I am sure we all admire the completed chair upholstered in a canvas-worked repeat pattern that complements the other embroideries in a needleworker's home.

The designs shown on page 52 are adapted from an old canvas-worked sampler. All are worked in Tent Stitches on #13 white mono-canvas. The original pieces were worked in Cross Stitches.

The intriguing scroll design at the lower right is a good example of how colors can create a feeling of motion in needlework. The contrast of dark and light blue against the reds and yellows creates a most unusual effect.

The dimensional effect of the design at the upper right would produce a dramatic carpet when worked in ponto grado with a solid black border to frame the pattern.

Small repeat designs are sometimes very monotonous and do not provide much opportunity for creative effects. The fruit motif at the upper left is an exceptionally choice small design. Notice the unusual background which is worked using two colors: white and light green in alternate rows of diagonal Basket Weave Stitch.

The leaf design at the lower left, worked in three shades of red with black, is suited to any color choice. It would be beautiful in blues and greens, and it could also be adapted for use as a repeat border.

Geometrical repeat designs are available in a canvas fabric called Pattern Weave. This material provides the needleworker with a perfectly spaced repeat design which is woven into the fabric and, therefore, does not require the counting of threads. Creative needleworkers have produced fascinating results with this material by changing the design, color, and use of stitches while relying on the basic design which is woven into the fabric.

Fleur-de-Lis repeat pattern was worked completely in Continuous Cross Stitches.

52   Four repeat designs were adapted from an old sampler.

Repeat designs make excellent borders as well as central motifs.

8. BARGELLO

Florentine canvas work, which is best known as Bargello, yields a variety of fascinating effects and consequently has many uses for upholstery and decorative adornment. Many patterns are available from records of the past, and modern yarn colors make it possible to achieve exciting new ideas in this canvas work. While this form of canvas work can be done in silks and cottons, the most effective pieces are worked in wools. For best results it is desirable to purchase yarn containing five shades of a color so that dimension and blending of tones can be accomplished.

Bargello canvas is woven of rough, coarse threads in a mono-weave. This 13-mesh canvas holds the stitch in position and produces better results than can be achieved on polished canvas of smooth threads.

All Bargello work is a definite repeat pattern achieved by counting the holes or threads of the canvas and therefore the stitch should not be confused with the Flame Stitch, which is worked irregularly, without accurate form. The diagram on page 50 has stitches placed over four threads of the canvas and indicates the needle passing under two threads, progressing upward and downward. Most designs are based on this four-thread count, but there are many patterns which require longer or shorter stitches. The famous Bargello pattern shown on page 55 creates a damask effect while forming a most unusual repeat design. It is important to notice that the stitch count in this design always places 2 long stitches below 2 short stitches.

Many Bargello patterns are based on historical examples and make striking, decorative upholstery as shown here.

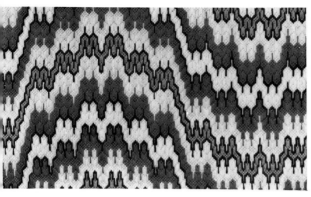

Above and right:
Cover design from the book *Bargello* by Elsa Williams. Adapted in wool from the original seventeenth-century chairs in the Museo Nazionale, Florence, Italy. This pattern was originally worked in silk threads.

9. REPRODUCTIONS

A reproduction of the
Sturbridge Village chair
seat on opposite page. The
size and shape of each
petal and leaf was care-
fully duplicated on #13
mono-canvas.

56

The original needlepoint chair seat found in the Old Sturbridge Village Collection in Sturbridge, Massachusetts, was worked in New England about 1740. This piece was done entirely in petit point.

Reproducing an old piece of needlework requires careful attention to color and form. Of course one does not copy damaged areas or badly faded colors, but it is important to keep very closely to the original work by examining the original yarn colors on the reverse side where it has been protected from fading. In many cases, the original colors on the back are extremely bright and the faded colors on the front have become soiled and dull. When this occurs it is best to compromise and use tones of color which appear old but which are related to both front and back colors.

It is extremely difficult to copy old pieces by counting stitches because faded colors and worn areas confuse the shapes and forms. To copy an old piece, it is easier to trace the pattern, transfer it onto the canvas and work the design by following the original for color and shading. Some museums allow you to place the original piece under glass so you can trace the pattern. This method of working the design permits the needleworker to change the mesh size of the canvas to accommodate one's own skill and eyesight.

Motifs adapted from the Sturbridge Village chair seat were worked on #10 duo-canvas.

This carpet was worked in sections. All the canvas pieces were carefully joined, and Basket Weave Stitches were used to conceal all seams.

When planning to join squares of a carpet or sections of canvas work, it is best to work the design on duo-canvas. The double-thread weave makes it easier to join the canvas sections smoothly by sewing backstitches between the threads, after carefully placing one canvas on top of the other so that the holes and threads of each match. When the seam is pressed open, the holes of the joined canvases will be perfectly aligned and one thread from each canvas section will produce a perfectly spaced double thread.

It is possible to join mono-canvas but it requires careful attention to the cross-weave of the canvas. Fold back a seam allowance along a single thread on each section of canvas. Make certain that the weave matches when the pieces are placed edge to edge as shown on page 60. Lace the two canvases together with a needle and thread, catching every other cross-thread that does not lie over the crease line thread (see the series of photographs on the next page). At the end of the seam, stitch the same lacing in the opposite direction, forming a cross stitch. Keep all stitches tight. Work this same cross-stitch lacing on the back side of the seam.

To produce invisible seams in a solid-colored area, it is best to use diagonal Basket Weave Stitches covering at least three stitches beyond each side of the seam allowance. Stitch through both thicknesses of canvas, matching the holes and concealing the cut edges of the canvas.

Dental floss is excellent for joining heavy, coarse canvas; strong, linen thread should be used for finer mesh.

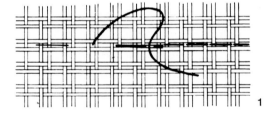

1

2

JOINING DUO-CANVAS:

1. Placing one canvas on top of the other, match the holes and stitch through both pieces of canvas with backstitches between the double threads.

2. The two sections of canvas are joined with Basket Weave Stitches covering the seam after canvas seam allowance is pressed open on reverse side.

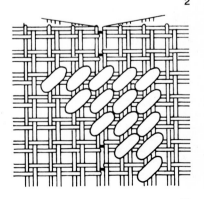

JOINING MONO-CANVAS:

1. Back of two sections of canvas with needle in position for lacing.

2. Lacing of seam completed on front of canvas.

3. Back of canvas with seam allowance trimmed to four threads on each side of seam line. Also shown is reverse side of Basket Weave Stitch used for joining.

4. Front of joined canvas shows perfect matching of canvas and smooth Basket Weave Stitches extended beyond canvas seam.

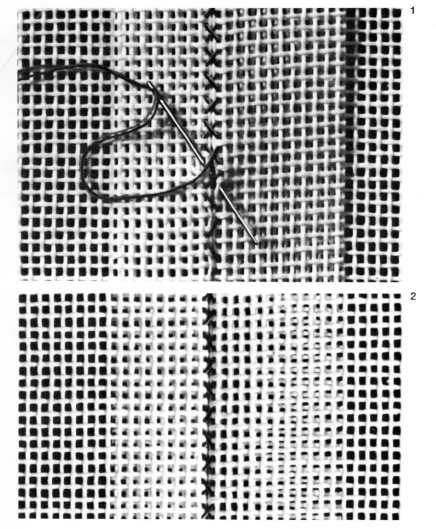

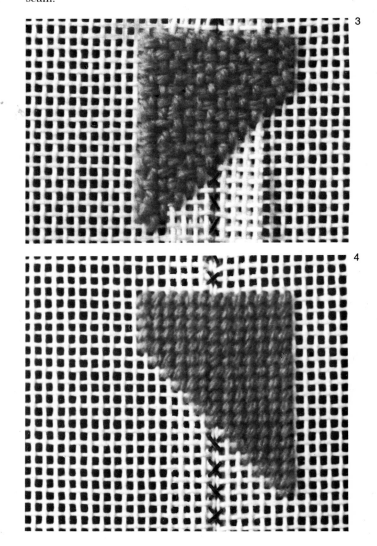

If the completed piece was worked on a needlepoint rod with soft, gentle stitches, it may require very little blocking. Usually a light pressing is all that is necessary for a smoothly worked piece. To iron the canvas work, place it right side down on a padded surface and cover it with a wet pressing cloth before applying the iron; or use a steam iron on a dry pressing cloth. If the piece has become flimsy and you wish to restore the stiffness of the canvas, use a muslin pressing cloth which has been dampened in salted, soapy water. Old-fashioned yellow naphtha soap is best for this.

To block a distorted piece is quite another matter, because blocking a canvas means restoring the weave of the canvas to its original position. If you have pulled it out of shape, you will now need to coax it back into shape. If the piece has textured or surface stitching, it should not be pressed with an iron. Instead, it is best to pin or staple the work on a blocking board that permits fast drying from both sides simultaneously.

How to Make a Blocking Board

For best results, make the base of your blocking board from a piece of insulation board. The cellulose type is best because pins and staples can be inserted and removed easily. Do not use any wooden board, plywood, or plasterboard. Your lumber dealer or hardware supplier has insulated wallboard in sheets 4 by 8 feet. Ask him to cut it to the sizes you need. One sheet will provide you with the following desirable sizes: 4 by 4 feet, 2 by 4 feet, and two pieces cut 2 by 2 feet. You will be able to block hundreds of pieces on these sections, using them over and over again.

The wallboard should be covered with clean, heavy, white muslin or drill cloth similar to what is used for ironing-board covers. With a staple gun, tack down the cover around the outside edges, making certain that the cloth is pulled taut. This must be done with care because this fabric will be permanently attached to the board. If you do not have a staple gun, you can use rust-free thumbtacks. Dampen the entire cloth lightly with a wet sponge to shrink the fabric so it is really tight across the board. Dry thoroughly.

Using a waterproof pen and a ruler, draw a horizontal line across the center of the fabric-covered board. Using a triangle or a compass, draw a vertical line through the horizontal one, dividing the board exactly into fourths. Keeping the lines at right angles, add parallel cross-lines 2 inches apart until the entire board is covered in 2-inch squares. These lines will be your guidelines for blocking various sizes of finished pieces time after time. When not in use, this permanent blocking board should be stored with the cloth attached.

To block a finished canvas, place it with the *right side of the needlework face down* on the blocking board. Arrange the piece so that the canvas threads are parallel to the inked lines of the board. Pin the corners temporarily for position. Staple or tack one side of the canvas piece along an inked guideline, pulling the piece flat and smooth at the same time. Tack the opposite side in the same way, this time pulling the piece smooth but not too tight. Tack the remaining two sides, beginning at the middle and working outward to the corners until all the edges are firm and smoothly applied. Remove the temporary pins at the corners.

With a wet sponge or a clean cloth, wet the entire canvas with naphtha-soap water to which salt or white vinegar has been added. Be sure to moisten both the canvas and the thread or yarn thoroughly and evenly. Allow the canvas piece to dry in an upright position for twenty-four hours before re-

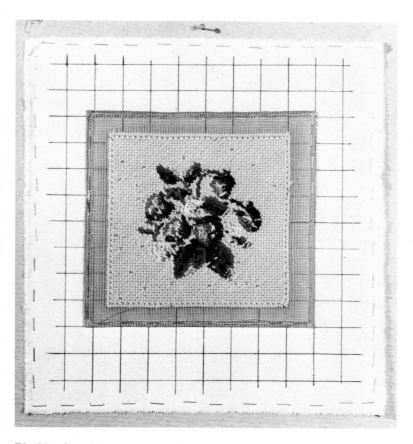

Blocking board has canvas work tacked right side down on the mounted cloth.

When finished, the canvas work can be framed. This canvas has bright yellow and orange flowers against a deep purple background. The white mat is also worked in needlepoint with light gray shadows in the lower section to create an effect of flower petals coming out of the picture.

moving it from the board. The mounting cloth and the porous cellulose board will absorb some moisture and provide air-drying on both sides of the piece at the same time.

All blocking should be done with the right side of the needlework placed face down on the blocking cloth so that the stitches are not disturbed nor rubbed with the sponge. When tufting stitches or high pile effects are included, it is better to block the needlework right side up and moisten the piece with a fine spray instead of a sponge.

When moistening a very large piece, the edges should first be well-dampened on all four sides to prevent its shrinking in any one direction. Continue moistening toward the center of the piece. Since large projects absorb more water and become heavy, it is best to dry them in a horizontal position. If this is not possible, be sure to reverse the upright board during the first hour so that all edges can dry evenly and water marks are avoided.

This excellent method of blocking can be used for all wool embroidery and for needlepoint. It is, of course, not practical to block most wearing apparel. For garments and extremely large items, pressing the piece on the wrong side with a steam iron, rather than pinning it to a blocking board, is preferable. Place Turkish toweling under the piece, with the embroidery face down. Do not allow the full weight of the iron to fall on the embroidery as it will crease the wool fibrils of the thread and create distortion in the stitches.

Do not wash canvas work. If the piece has become soiled, have it dry-cleaned, but request that ironing or pressing be omitted. Commercial pressing will set the fibers of the wool and make it very difficult to block the piece properly thereafter.

If the piece you are blocking is hand-painted, *be sure* to use salt or vinegar in the water used for dampening the pressing cloth. Never soak the canvas piece in water.

I have never been able to understand why anyone would want to bathe their needlework. However, if you are an advocate of the treatment using cold-water soap, please, please, do add vinegar or salt to prevent possible discharge of color.

Pieces which are severely distorted will, of course, be held in alignment when they are upholstered or tacked to a mounting board. However, distorted pieces which are not later mounted to a firm surface sometimes refuse to hold their shape after blocking. Rabbit skin glue is helpful for most of these pieces. This gelatin-like substance is purchased in powder form and when congealed is applied to the back of the canvas work *while* the piece is pinned or stapled to the blocking board. Pillows and bellpulls usually require less stiffening than carpets. Since this glue is water-soluble, it must be replaced if the carpet is cleaned. Do not try to use any rubber-based carpet backing on needleworked carpets. The chemical content of latex glues affects the dyes of the wool yarns unfavorably and causes discoloration.

Almost all tapestry wools and crewels are protected with mothproofing compounds but, if there is doubt when using unlabeled yarns, one should always spray the finished piece with a mothproofing solution. The use of a soil-resistant spray, which is available in aerosol cans, is advisable for all pieces that might be soiled while in use.

When framing pictures, it is best to mount the canvas work on thin plywood before framing, making certain that the weave of the canvas is squarely placed on the edge of the wood. Canvas-work pictures are always more beautiful without a glass covering.

INDEX

(Numbers in bold face indicate the pages on which stitch diagrams appear.)

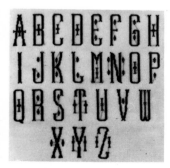

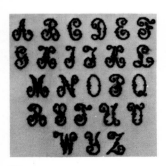

These examples of lettering are from the book *Alphabets and Designs*, by Doris Drake, which contains 35 different styles of letters suitable for canvas work.